ASIA

Alexis Roumanis

www.av2books.com

LET'S READ

AV²
BY WEIGL™

ADDED VALUE • AUDIO VISUAL

Go to **www.av2books.com**, and enter this book's unique code.

BOOK CODE

U487554

AV² by Weigl brings you media enhanced books that support active learning.

AV² provides enriched content that supplements and complements this book. Weigl's AV² books strive to create inspired learning and engage young minds in a total learning experience.

Your AV² Media Enhanced books come alive with...

Audio
Listen to sections of the book read aloud.

Video
Watch informative video clips.

Embedded Weblinks
Gain additional information for research.

Try This!
Complete activities and hands-on experiments.

Key Words
Study vocabulary, and complete a matching word activity.

Quizzes
Test your knowledge.

Slide Show
View images and captions, and prepare a presentation.

... and much, much more!

Published by AV² by Weigl
350 5th Avenue, 59th Floor New York, NY 10118
Websites: www.av2books.com   www.weigl.com

Library of Congress Cataloging-in-Publication Data

Roumanis, Alexis.
 Asia / Alexis Roumanis.
     pages cm. -- (Exploring continents)
Includes bibliographical references and index.
ISBN 978-1-4896-3030-8 (hard cover : alk. paper) -- ISBN 978-1-4896-3031-5 (soft cover : alk. paper) --
ISBN 978-1-4896-3032-2 (single user ebook) -- ISBN 978-1-4896-3033-9 (multi-user ebook)
1. Asia--Juvenile literature. I. Title.
DS5.R68 2014
950--dc23

                                 2014044123

Printed in the United States of America in Brainerd, Minnesota
1 2 3 4 5 6 7 8 9 0 18 17 16 15 14

122014   Project Coordinator: Jared Siemens
WEP051214   Design: Mandy Christiansen

Weigl acknowledges iStock and Getty Images as the primary image suppliers for this title.

ASIA

Contents

Welcome to Asia.
It is the largest continent.

This is the shape of Asia.
Europe lies to the
west of Asia.
Australia and
Antarctica sit
to the south.

Where Is Asia?

Arctic Ocean

Arctic Ocean

North America

Europe

ASIA

Pacific Ocean

Atlantic Ocean

Africa

Pacific Ocean

South America

Indian Ocean

Australia

N
W E
S

Antarctica

Three oceans touch
the coast of Asia.

Asia is made up of many different landforms. Deserts, mountains, plains, and rainforests can all be found in Asia.

The Yangtze River is the longest river in Asia.

The Caspian Sea is the world's largest salt lake.

The Gobi Desert is the largest desert in Asia.

Mount Everest is the tallest mountain in the world.

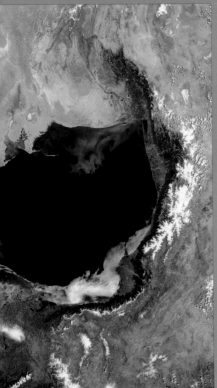

Lake Baikal is the deepest lake in the world.

Asia is home to some of the most unique animals in the world. Many different kinds of animals live there.

There are less than 10,000 adult red pandas left in nature.

The fastest land animal in Asia is the blackbuck.

Asia is home to many different types of plants.

The flowers of a fig tree are found inside its fruit.

Bamboo can grow up to 130 feet (40 meters) high.

A cypress tree in Iran is the oldest tree in Asia. It is 4,000 years old.

More people eat rice
than any other food
in the world.

Orange trees first
came from Asia.

China is one of the oldest countries in Asia. It is more than 4,000 years old. People have lived in Asia for thousands of years.

The Naga are one of the first peoples of Asia.

Many kinds of people live in Asia. Each group of people is special in its own way.

Hmong women in China wear silver jewelry during festivals.

Japanese samurai wore special armor to keep them safe.

More than 4.3 billion people live in Asia. The country with the most land in Asia is China.

More people live in Tokyo, Japan, than in any other city in the world.

There are many things that can be found only in Asia. People come from all over the world to visit this continent.

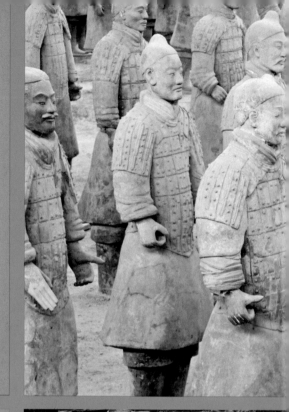

The Great Wall of China is more than 5,000 miles (8,000 kilometers) long.

It took more than 2,000 years to build the Banaue Rice Terraces in the Philippines.

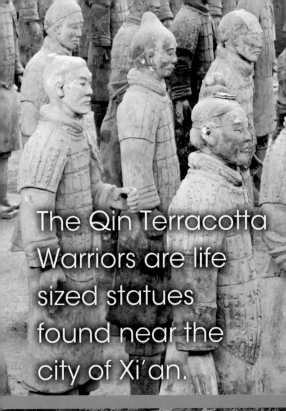

The Potala Palace in Tibet was built more than 1,400 years ago.

The Qin Terracotta Warriors are life sized statues found near the city of Xi'an.

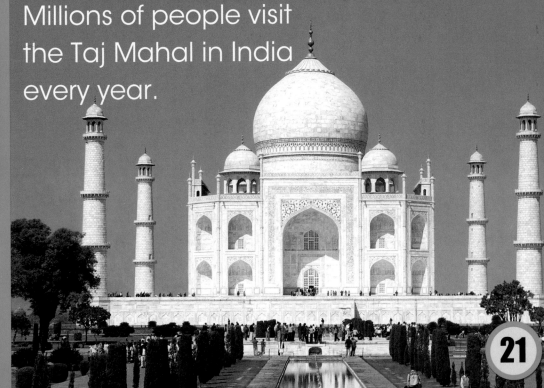

Millions of people visit the Taj Mahal in India every year.

Asia Quiz

See what you have learned about the continent of Asia.

What do these pictures tell you about Asia?

KEY WORDS

Research has shown that as much as 65 percent of all written material published in English is made up of 300 words. These 300 words cannot be taught using pictures or learned by sounding them out. They must be recognized by sight. This book contains 75 common sight words to help young readers improve their reading fluency and comprehension. This book also teaches young readers several important content words, such as proper nouns. These words are paired with pictures to aid in learning and improve understanding.

Page	Sight Words First Appearance
4	is, it, the, to
7	and, of, this, three, where
8	all, be, can, different, found, in, made, many, mountains, river, sea, up, world
10	animal
11	are, home, kinds, land, left, live, most, some, than, there
12	a, feet, grow, high, its, old, plants, tree, years
13	any, came, eat, first, food, from, more, other, people
15	for, have, one
16	each, group, keep, them
17	often
19	city, country, with
20	come, great, life, long, miles, near, only, over, that, things, took
21	every, was

Page	Content Words First Appearance
4	Asia, continent
7	Antarctica, Australia, coast, Europe, oceans, shape
8	deserts, lake, landforms, plains, rainforests
10	cat, elephant, Komodo dragon, lizard, tiger
11	blackbuck, nature, red pandas
12	bamboo, flowers, fruit, Iran
13	orange, rice
15	China, Naga
16	armor, festivals, jewelry, samurai, women
17	cloths, monks, robes, saris, Thailand
19	Japan, Tokyo
20	Philippines, statues, Xi'an
21	India, Tibet

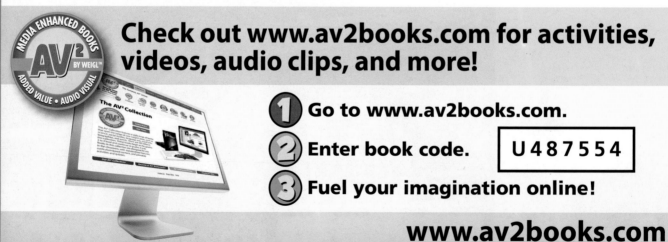